REAL ESTATE Legacy

A Father-Son Journey

Real Estate Legacy: *A Father-Son Journey*

FIRST EDITION
Published by T J INVESTORS

www.TJInvestors.com

ISBN: 979-8-218-64027-9
Library of Congress Cataloging-in-Publication Data

Library of Congress Case
Barney, Wesley and Barney, Tyrek
Real Estate Legacy: A Father-Son Journey
Case Number: 1-14902126313| April 2025

Category: Self-Help, Real Estate, Investment, Legacy, Financial Literacy

Authors: Wesley Barney | BunkeyBarney@gmail.com
Tyrek Barney | TyrekBarney@gmail.com

Editor: Jaclyn Shultz | Jaclyn.AShultz@gmail.com

Cover Designer & Prep for Publishing: EliJah Blyden Sr.| www.EliTheBookGuy.com

Printed in the United States of America by Book Bindery: A&A Printing & Publishing | www.PrintShopCentral.com

DISCLAIMER

The statements made about products and services have not been evaluated by the U.S. government. Please consult with your own legal and accounting professional regarding the suggestions and recommendations made in this book.

Except as specifically stated in this book, neither the author or publisher, nor authors, contributors or other representatives will be liable for damages arising out of or in connection with the use of this book. This is a comprehensive limitation of liability that applies to all damages of any kind, including (without limitation) compensatory, direct, indirect or consequential damages; loss of data, income or profit; loss of or damage to property and claims of third parties.

You understand that this book is not intended as a substitute for consultation with a licensed legal or accounting professional. Before you begin any change in your lifestyle in any way, you will consult a licensed professional to ensure you are doing what is best for your situation.

To our families,
for their endless love and sacrifices.

To our mentors,
for their wisdom and guidance.

To those who dare to dream,
take risks, and bet on themselves—this book is for you.
May it inspire you to learn, grow, and build something that lasts.

PREFACE

This book is for anyone looking to create financial independence through real estate investing. Whether you're a beginner trying to understand the fundamentals, an investor looking to refine your strategy, or someone seeking inspiration to take the leap, this book provides real, actionable insights from our personal journeys.

It's for:

- **Aspiring Investors** – Those ready to get into real estate but unsure of where to start.
- **Seasoned Investors** – Those who want to sharpen their skills, expand their strategies, or avoid common pitfalls.
- **Entrepreneurs & Business Owners** – Anyone looking to leverage real estate as a wealth-building vehicle.
- **Legacy Builders** – Those who want to create generational wealth, not just for themselves but for their families and communities.

This isn't just a how-to book—it's a **blueprint** for taking action, overcoming setbacks, and playing the long game in real estate. If you're ready to step up and build something meaningful, then this book is for you.

CONTENTS

PART IV
CHALLENGES AND TRIUMPHS

PART V
THE GOOD WITH THE BAD

PART VI
ADVANCED STRATEGIES & LESSONS

REAL ESTATE *Legacy*

A FATHER-SON JOURNEY

BY WESLEY & TYREK BARNEY

Introduction

Welcome to our journey through the world of real estate—a journey marked by humble beginnings, persistent growth, and a relentless pursuit of excellence. This memoir is more than just a guide for real estate investors; it's a story of ambition, resilience, and the powerful bond between a father and son.

Our story begins in a small, middle-class family where the seeds of real estate were planted early. My father, a determined and resourceful investor, introduced me to the world of property investment at a young age. What makes our journey unique is the dynamic of a father-son partnership—two generations working together to build something lasting. Our relationship has been tested and strengthened through the challenges and triumphs of real estate, and we hope our story resonates not only with investors but also with those who value family, mentorship, and perseverance.

This book serves multiple audiences. For aspiring real estate investors, it provides insights into getting started, making strategic decisions, and navigating the inevitable obstacles. For seasoned investors, it offers lessons from our experiences, highlighting both our successes and mistakes. Beyond the realm of real estate, this book is also for those who are interested in the dynamics of a father-son relationship, the passing down of knowledge, and the generational impact of a shared vision.

One distinctive aspect of this book is its format. Some chapters are written from my perspective, while others are authored by my father. This dual narrative provides insight into our unique experiences and perspectives, allowing readers to see the evolution of our investment strategies and the invaluable lessons passed down between generations.

Whether you're here to gain real estate knowledge, explore the nuances of family business dynamics, or simply enjoy an engaging story of growth and transformation, we welcome you. Join us as we explore the foundations of our real estate journey, the pivotal moments that defined our path, and the enduring principles that continue to guide us. This is our legacy, and we're excited to share it with you.

PART I

Foundations

CHAPTER 1

Seeds of Real Estate

– Tyrek Barney

I grew up in your typical middle-class, hardworking family. Our family dynamic was like a comedy sketch—maybe not always pretty, but certainly memorable. My parents were a dynamic duo of co-parenting. Was it always harmonious? Well, let's just say we had our fair share of sitcom-worthy moments. But what family is perfect anyway? My mother and father were exceptionally committed to raising my brothers and me. They valued their children more than anything else, and boy, did they let us know it. Their love was felt throughout my entire childhood—even their tough love, which, looking back, I now appreciate as character-building boot camp. I count myself fortunate and blessed to have had such incredible parents, their unwavering love, and their endless support. Without them, I wouldn't be who I am today.

My exposure to the world of real estate in my childhood was primarily through my father. He was a real estate enthusiast with investment properties scattered throughout New York at the time. My dad wasn't one to shy away from a little sweat equity. In fact, he roped my brothers and me into helping him with clean-outs, laying down flooring, and demo work. He called it "bonding time," but we quickly learned he was just trying to save a buck—though, to his credit, he did pay us. At the time, I thought I was just earning a few bucks. But in reality, I was gaining hands-on experience that would later become second nature when I started my own real estate ventures.

Ah, the teenage years—a time when my brothers wanted nothing to do with our parents, especially not babysitting their baby brother. Lucky for me, that meant I got to embark on weekend adventures with Dad. Our destination: Syracuse, New York, a place that would forever be etched in my memory.

Syracuse had a way of making an impression, not just because of the freezing winters but because of what it represented in my journey. Our weekends there involved a routine that left a lasting mark on me. We would wake up early, load into the car with coffee in hand (hot chocolate for me), and drive around the city, collecting rent, checking on tenants, and participating in the age-old practice of "driving for dollars". This meant navigating neighborhoods in search of vacant or distressed properties—the ones with overgrown lawns, peeling paint, or broken windows.

The neighborhoods themselves told a story. Some blocks showcased well-maintained houses with trimmed lawns, while others were dotted with abandoned buildings, graffiti-covered storefronts, and homes in dire need of repair. The contrast between revitalized areas and those still struggling with neglect was striking. The air carried a mix of fresh pavement, crisp morning chill, and the occasional scent of home-cooked meals wafting from apartment windows. Sidewalks bustled with children playing and families trying to make the best of their circumstances.

The properties that piqued my dad's interest were documented with an old Polaroid camera. He'd slow the car down just enough for me to snap a photo, then we'd jot down the address in his worn-out notebook. These small but significant tasks made me feel like I had a role, like I was part of something important. There was a rhythm to it all—an unspoken understanding between my dad and me as we surveyed each street, each property, and speculated on their potential. I didn't realize it at the time, but those weekends were shaping my perspective on work ethic, investment, and the power of seeing opportunities where others saw problems.

Beyond real estate, those trips were about more than just business. They were about lessons, about the quiet moments of wisdom that my father shared between collecting rent and making small talk with tenants. He taught me how to assess a neighborhood's potential, how to see beyond a property's exterior flaws, and most importantly, how to connect with people. We weren't just dealing with buildings; we were dealing with lives, with families trying to make ends meet.

Those early experiences in Syracuse did more than cultivate my interest in real estate—they instilled in me the value of hard work, dedication, and the importance of forging strong bonds with family. They laid the foundation for the real estate journey that would unfold in the chapters to come.

CHAPTER 2

Starting from Scratch

– Wesley Barney

My journey in the real estate investing world started back in 1988. Like many folks, I was broke and had poor credit. I was married, living with my grandmother in her house in Queens, New York, with two kids at the time. A couple of months later, we finally moved out of my grandmother's house and into a Section 8 apartment building.

At first, it was nice that we had our own apartment. However, after six months, I knew I had to get out of there. We had so many mice in the apartment, people hanging out late at night in front of the building selling crack, and human feces in the stairwell. I had a job doing security from 3:00 p.m. to 11:00 p.m. Every time I came home at night, there was always a crowd of people hanging out in the lobby. We complained to management, but it seemed to fall on deaf ears.

One night, I was watching television, and a real estate infomercial came on, saying you too can be rich through real estate investing or buy your own house with 3% down. At that point in my life, I would do anything to get out of that apartment building, as long as it was legal. That message appealed to me. I started dreaming about owning real estate with cash flow and owning my own house, so I purchased their program. I think it was Tom Vu or Dave Del Dotto back in those days. Once I received their course material, I did a deep dive into studying, reading real estate books every day for about four months.

I became so obsessed with real estate investing because I hated where I lived. I was motivated and determined to get my family out of that environment. The course material recommended that you join a local real estate investors association, which I did in New York City. I liked listening to this real estate radio talk show host, Sonny Block, from whom I learned a lot, though he was later indicted for tax evasion, bilking investors out of $21 million.

In 1990, I continued to attend the real estate club meetings. One night at the meeting, I met an attorney who had some properties he was selling in Central Islip, New York. I approached him about the property he was selling, and he gave me the address. My ex-wife at the time and I went to see the property. It was a corner property, a gable-style house, two stories with a basement. He only wanted $5,000 down.

Needless to say, I did not have $5,000, but we had at least $2,500, and my grandmother gifted me $4,500 (bless her heart). We went through the whole process: signed the contract, qualified for a HUD mortgage, and did a home inspection. When we went to the closing and I looked at the closing statement, my attorney said a certain portion went to the owner. His net proceeds were $80,000.

My ex-wife started crying. She was overwhelmed—seeing those numbers on the paperwork made everything feel real. We had just made the biggest financial commitment of our lives, and the reality of it hit her hard. The weight of responsibility, the fear of the unknown, and the realization that we were stepping into something we had never done before all rushed in at once. We were putting everything we had on the line for this opportunity, and it felt like a sink-or-swim moment.

Then, I looked at the numbers again. The seller had owned this property for over fifteen years. He had likely paid a fraction of what we were buying it for and had collected rental income on top of that. Now, he was walking away with a check for $80,000. That was life-changing money for us at the time, and he was making it off one transaction. It hit me like a ton of bricks—this was how investors really made their money.

Reading about real estate deals in books was one thing, but sitting across the table from someone profiting off a property they had held onto for years gave me an entirely new perspective. It wasn't just about finding a property and buying it—it was about time, leverage, and knowing when to sell. I realized I had been on the wrong side of the equation my entire life. That experience changed me. I wasn't just buying a house; I was getting an education in wealth-building, and I was determined to be the one on the other side of that table in the future.

I was so angry and motivated at the same time. That moment lit a fire within me, pushing me to take control of my financial future. I made a decision at that moment: I was going to become a real estate investor. I would not just be a buyer. I would learn how to acquire, hold, and sell for a profit. This was no longer just about moving my family into a house—it was about changing our financial trajectory forever.

Three years later, things gradually started to change for me mentally. Those late nights I spent reading, studying, listening to real estate tapes, visiting properties, networking, attending seminars, and workshops were paying off. My self-confidence and belief in myself were growing. I started buying foreclosures and tax deed properties part-time, plus I got a job with the New York City Fire Department. Things started looking up for me. I was invited to share my experience at the investors' real estate meetings. I also started sharing my experiences at community colleges and universities in their adult continuing education courses.

In 1995, I started a real estate investors association called Ultimate Investors Real Estate Inc. I was also invited to do an infomercial with John Beck on buying properties for "Pennies on the Dollar." I have helped hundreds of students buy tax deed properties and mortgage foreclosures. I have purchased foreclosure properties in New York City, Syracuse, New York, New Jersey, Tulsa, Oklahoma, Kansas City, Missouri, and Florida.

The best part of my success is sharing my experience with my youngest son. He may not have realized it at the time, but those weekends spent picking up rent checks and fixing houses were shaping him, just like they shaped me. There was a little pushback because he loved to play football, like any other kid. I get it as a dad. But years later, it came so naturally to him.

After he graduated from college, he started buying tax certificates, tax deed properties, and foreclosures. Later in the book, he will share his experience. For now, I am going to take you on my real estate journey on how to buy foreclosure properties and make a fortune.

PART II

The Growth Phase

CHAPTER 3

Learning the Ropes

– Wesley Barney

In my early days of real estate investing, I faced numerous challenges and learned many lessons that shaped my journey. One of the most significant lessons was the importance of self-education. I immersed myself in books, seminars, and workshops, absorbing as much knowledge as possible. This foundation of knowledge gave me the confidence to take calculated risks and make informed decisions.

Another crucial lesson was the value of networking. Through real estate club meetings, I found money private lenders who were willing to team up with me to buy foreclosure properties at auctions. This access to capital was a game-changer, allowing me to take advantage of deals that would have otherwise been out of reach. It's a strategy I still use today—leveraging relationships to create financial opportunities that benefit everyone involved.

Persistence was key. Real estate investing is not a get-rich-quick scheme. It requires dedication, hard work, and patience. There were times when I faced setbacks and obstacles, but I never gave up. Another major lesson came when I purchased a property in Syracuse at a public auction. They only required 5%

down, with the remaining balance due in 30 days. It seemed like a great deal—until I contacted my attorney to conduct a title report. He informed me that the property had numerous liens, violations, and that the previous owner had passed away. His advice was clear: Do not proceed with the purchase. However, by that point, I had already sent a FedEx package containing a $75,000 check for the remaining payment.

Realizing the mistake, I hustled back to FedEx, desperate to retrieve that envelope before it was sent out. Luck was on my side—I managed to get it back, avoiding what could have been a financial disaster. In the end, I only lost my $2,500 deposit, but the lesson was invaluable: Always conduct due diligence ahead of time. Had I gone through with that deal, I would have inherited a mess of legal and financial troubles. This experience reinforced the importance of patience and thorough research before jumping into any investment.

Lastly, I learned the importance of giving back. Sharing my knowledge and experiences with others not only helped them succeed but also reinforced my own understanding. Teaching and mentoring aspiring investors became a fulfilling aspect of my journey. I started mentoring a young investor who reminded me of myself—hungry to learn but unsure where to start. I helped him analyze his first deal, guiding him through the negotiation process and ensuring he didn't make the same rookie mistakes I did. Watching him successfully close his first property and later expand his portfolio reaffirmed that real estate is more than just financial gain; it's about building relationships and empowering others.

Each lesson, each connection, and each challenge I faced in those early years contributed to the investor I became. The road wasn't always smooth, but every rough patch added to my understanding of how to navigate the business. And as I continued forward, I knew that the knowledge I gained wasn't just for me—it was meant to be shared, to help others carve their own paths in real estate.

CHAPTER 4

From Campus to Corporate

– Tyrek Barney

College life was a whirlwind of excitement, and I was living it to the fullest. I had bid farewell to my dreams of NFL stardom and shifted my focus to track and field. Pursuing a degree in business finance was my new game plan, and I was racing toward the finish line of graduation. During my college years, real estate wasn't even a blip on my radar. I was your quintessential student-athlete, juggling books and weights while trying to maintain some semblance of a social life. It was a time of epic campus adventures and late-night pizza feasts. But as the saying goes, you can only have so much fun before you start wondering about your purpose in this world.

Like many fresh graduates, I had high hopes for what came next. I envisioned myself thriving in corporate America, putting my finance degree to work, learning from seasoned professionals, and eventually climbing the ranks. My first job out of college was in the financial sector, and I stayed within the industry for many years, gaining massive experience and exposure working for different firms. It seemed like the logical step—good salary, benefits, and the promise of career growth. But the reality of corporate life set in quickly.

One memory from my corporate days still has me chuckling even now. I was summoned to my manager's office, fully expecting a gold star for my hard work and dedication. But what awaited me was a conversation about oatmeal. Yes, you read that right—oatmeal. Apparently, my office snacking habits were affecting "office optics." The look on my face was a masterpiece of bewilderment. I couldn't help but wonder, "Is this for real?" However, I chose to keep my humor in check and replied with a straight face, "Okay, it won't happen again." Deep down, I knew that oatmeal was the least of my worries in the grand scheme of cubicle conundrums.

It was around this time that my perspective started to shift. Being exposed to finance in general opened my eyes. Working for large financial corporations, I began to understand different financial products and financial planning on a deeper level. I started seeing how wealth was created and protected, not just for individuals, but for businesses and institutions.

This knowledge merged with my dad's constant conversations about real estate. The more I listened, the more it made sense. My exposure to finance and my dad's experience started to blend together, forming a clearer picture of what I wanted for my own future. I wasn't just thinking about escaping corporate life—I was thinking about finding my purpose. That required deep self-reflection, and I started looking back at the things that had excited me as a kid. The freedom of entrepreneurship, the ability to create and build, and the idea of being in control of my own financial destiny all resonated with me. That's when I knew real estate wasn't just something my dad did—it was something I could do, too. Corporate America wasn't turning out to be the fulfilling experience I had anticipated. I was working long hours, but something was missing. That's when my dad's voice became a guiding presence in my life. Our conversations were filled with wisdom, humor, and an undeniable push toward something bigger than a paycheck.

In those moments of professional frustration, I sought solace in conversations with my dad. His words were pure gold, sprinkled with wisdom and delivered with a warm smile. It's a language he continues to speak to this very day. During those moments, he wasn't merely uttering words; he was nurturing the seeds of entrepreneurship that had taken root within me. He had walked in my shoes, experienced the same thoughts and frustrations, and he understood the journey like no one else could.

There were moments when he'd catch me while I was on the train to work, and he'd ask with a chuckle, "Yo Rek, what you doing? You on that slave train?" or, "On your way to the plantation?" His humor was both endearing and thought-provoking. And when he used that word, "Boyyy," it was like a portal to the past, invoking memories of stories he'd shared about how his grandfather addressed him.

But beneath the humor, my dad was spot on. The reality was clear—I wasn't meant to spend my life in a cubicle. I often laughed when he'd tell me that, not because it was funny, but because it was undeniably true. It was time for me to take control of my life, put plans into action, and break free from the corporate mold. That realization didn't come overnight, but little by little, the idea of real estate—the world my dad had lived and breathed for decades—started to make more sense. It wasn't just an option; it was an opportunity to build something of my own.

PART III

The Entrepreneurial Spark

CHAPTER 5

Finding My Path

– Tyrek Barney

With my father's words echoing in my mind, I began to seriously consider my next steps. The corporate life, with its oatmeal conversations and endless meetings, was no longer enough for me. I realized I wanted something more—something that would allow me to be my own boss and make a tangible impact.

It started small. I began reading books and articles about real estate investment in my spare time. The more I learned, the more excited I became. I remembered those weekends in Syracuse with my dad, the thrill of identifying potential properties, and the satisfaction of seeing a project come to life. It all started to make sense. Real estate wasn't just a passing interest from my childhood; it was a potential career path.

But taking the leap wasn't easy. Reading about real estate was one thing—actually buying a property was another. I hesitated, wondering if I was making the right decision. What if I failed? What if I lost my savings? I spent weeks analyzing potential properties, crunching numbers, and watching market trends. Finally, I found one that felt right—a single-family townhome, two-bedroom, one-bath, in a decent neighborhood. Unlike the distressed properties I had been researching, this one was move-in ready with no major maintenance needed—a solid first buy for someone starting out. The goal was to use it as a rental property, generating steady income over time.

I took out a conventional 30-year mortgage, putting down a $15,000 down payment using the savings I had amassed from my corporate job. It was a big commitment, but I saw it as an investment in my future. To this day, I still own the property, and it continues to serve as a rental, proving to be one of the best decisions I made early in my real estate journey. It was affordable, had good bones, and was in an area where I saw potential for growth.

Those early days were tough—juggling my day job and managing the rental property was exhausting. Unexpected repair costs popped up, tenants had issues, and neighbors would call me to complain about them. There were nights I questioned if I had made a mistake, but I had to ignore those thoughts. I reminded myself that real estate investing isn't about short-term wins—it's about long-term wealth building. Success wouldn't come overnight, but I was in it for the long haul.

From that point on, there was no looking back. I continued to invest in real estate, each property teaching me something new. I learned to navigate the complexities of real estate transactions, manage contractors more efficiently, and understand market trends. With each success, my confidence grew, and so did my vision for the future.

Real estate investing became more than just a business; it became a passion. I began to see the potential for larger projects and more significant impacts. My journey was just beginning, and I was ready to embrace the challenges and opportunities that lay ahead.

As I continued to build my real estate portfolio, I never forgot the lessons from my childhood or the wisdom of my father. His guidance and the experiences we shared were the foundation of my success. I was no longer just a corporate employee or a house flipper—I was a real estate developer, an entrepreneur, and a man on a mission to create something meaningful.

The entrepreneurial spark had been ignited, and there was no extinguishing it. I was ready to take on the world, one property at a time.

CHAPTER 6

The Power of Foreclosures

– Wesley Barney

When I first dipped my toes into the vast ocean of real estate investing, I felt like a kid in a candy store—so many strategies, concepts, and techniques. Amid this sea of options, one concept stood out, waved its hands, and yelled, "Pick me!" That concept? Investing in foreclosures, baby! Whether it was mortgage foreclosures, trustee deed foreclosures, or tax deed foreclosure auctions, these were the cool kids on the real estate block, and I was determined to join their squad.

What Is a Foreclosure?

A foreclosure happens when a homeowner fails to keep up with their mortgage payments, typically for three to four months, leading the lender to take legal action to recover the unpaid loan balance. This process results in the property being repossessed and sold to recover the debt. Foreclosures present opportunities for investors to purchase properties below market value through various stages of the process.

The Three Phases of Foreclosures

There are three phases of foreclosures: pre-foreclosure, auction, and post-foreclosure (REO, or real estate owned). Each phase presents different opportunities for investors:

1. **Pre-Foreclosure** – This occurs when a homeowner falls behind on mortgage payments but still owns the property. Investors can negotiate directly with the homeowner to create win-win solutions before the property goes to auction. Because the homeowner is still in control, buyers can access the property for inspections and secure conventional financing through a bank, making it similar to buying a traditional home.

2. **Auction** – If the homeowner doesn't resolve the default, the property goes to auction. This phase carries higher risks but also higher rewards. Auctions require buyers to have cash on hand, as financing is not an option. Competition can be intense, but experienced investors who do their research can secure great deals below market value.

3. **Post-Foreclosure (REO)** – If no one bids on a property at auction, it becomes bank-owned. Investors can then negotiate directly with the bank, often securing favorable deals. Unlike auctions, financing options are available when purchasing REO properties, making them a viable option for those without large cash reserves.

One of my most memorable auction experiences was when I purchased 3521 Mersington. It was a trustee sale, taking place at 10 a.m. on the courthouse steps in Kansas City, Missouri. There was only one other bidder besides me. I remember standing there, heart pounding, as the auctioneer read the terms of the sale.

I had done my research beforehand, ensuring there were no hidden liens or legal issues, so I was prepared to bid with confidence. The auctioneer started the bidding, and the other bidder and I went back and forth, raising our hands, each trying to outmaneuver the other. The excitement and nerves were overwhelming. Then came the words: "Going once, going twice… sold!"

I had just purchased a house for $26,870—one that was worth $100,000 after some rehabilitation. Can you imagine buying a house for that price? The adrenaline rush of being the successful bidder is something every real estate investor should experience at least once. That deal reinforced why I loved foreclosure auctions.

Why invest in foreclosures? Well, imagine buying real estate at prices that make Black Friday sales look like a luxury department store on a regular Tuesday. We're talking 20%, 30%, even 40% below market value—it's like getting the latest gadget at half price, but better, because it's real estate, baby!

When you buy foreclosure properties, you're like a real estate ninja, making all-cash moves without the burden of mortgage payments. No traditional closing costs to rain on your parade, saving you thousands of dollars to spend on, you know, more real estate adventures! And once you've conquered the property, free and clear of all mortgages, the world is your oyster. You can flex your real estate muscles with various profitable strategies. Want a property for yourself? Done. Fancy fixing and renting it out? Easy peasy. How about flipping it for quick cash? You got it. Add value with some rehab magic and retail the property? Consider it done. Rent with the option to buy? Sure thing. Or why not become the bank with seller financing and create a mortgage note? The opportunities are as endless as a bottomless mimosa brunch.

For those just starting out, financing foreclosure deals without large capital is absolutely possible. If you're buying at auction, you'll need cash, but that doesn't mean you have to fund it alone. Some investors pool resources with family and friends, while others secure funding through hard money lenders—private lenders who finance deals with terms that favor speed over low interest rates. Hard money lenders are quick to fund your deal, but let's be real—those funds come with chains attached!

If you're buying a bank-owned property (REO), you have more financing options, including conventional mortgages and investment loans. The key is understanding creative financing and leveraging the right strategy for your situation.

As successful as foreclosures had been for us, the real estate world never stands still. Just as we were mastering one game, a new challenge emerged—one no investor could have predicted. The housing market shifted, and with it, new strategies were required to navigate the ever-changing landscape. In the later chapters, we'll explore how we adapted to these changes and continued to thrive in real estate investing.

PART IV

Challenges and Triumphs

CHAPTER 7

Adapting to a New Reality

– Tyrek Barney

The year 2020 brought unexpected challenges with the onset of the COVID-19 pandemic. Like many others, I found myself facing a world turned upside down. The pandemic affected every aspect of life, and the real estate market was no exception. Initially, the uncertainty and fear were overwhelming. Real estate transactions slowed, and projects were put on hold. For me, this meant potential deals I had been researching were no longer viable, and financing became more difficult to secure as lenders tightened their requirements. Renovation timelines stretched longer due to supply chain disruptions, and tenant issues became more complicated with eviction moratoriums in place. I felt stuck, questioning the stability of my career path.

But in every crisis, there is opportunity. With more people working from home and re-evaluating their living spaces, new trends in real estate began to emerge. This was a turning point for me, a chance to adapt and innovate.

I took a step back and re-evaluated my strategy. I approached my dad and told him I was ready to step up in the world of real estate. This was his opportunity to share his wealth of knowledge and years of experience. We talked about the different avenues I could pursue as a beginning investor. It was one of the biggest hurdles to navigate: Should I focus on Buy and Hold? Fix and Flip? Vacation Rentals? Development? The list seemed endless.

My dad introduced me to the strategy that had brought him major success: tax foreclosures. Simply put, if property taxes are delinquent, the property can be sold at a tax foreclosure sale—even if the mortgage has been paid in full. These sales are held once a year in every state, and the property is auctioned to the highest bidder. This seemed like a reasonable place to start because I didn't have a lot of money to play with in the Long Island/NYC metro area. My father suggested starting in Kansas City, Missouri—a city I had never been to before.

Leading up to the sale, which is held every August, we did all our due diligence and research. This involved flying to Kansas City for a weekend and driving around different zip codes and neighborhoods. That weekend, we saw over 200 properties easily. From eight in the morning until six at night for three straight days, we toured potential investments.

Kansas City was different from New York in many ways, yet there were certain similarities that made me feel oddly at ease. The streets were lined with single-family homes, some well-maintained, while others showed clear signs of neglect. There were neighborhoods with tree-lined streets, classic Midwestern charm, and well-kept brick houses, but just a few blocks over, you could find entire streets of boarded-up homes and overgrown yards. Unlike the dense, fast-paced environment of

New York, KC had a slower, more spread-out feel. Yet, the real estate opportunities were undeniable. Some areas reminded me of sections of Syracuse I had explored as a kid with my dad—pockets of potential waiting for the right investor to step in.

The crazy thing about that experience was that it felt like déjà vu, taking me back to my childhood when I used to drive around Syracuse with my dad looking at properties. Fast forward over a decade later, here we were, driving for dollars in Kansas City. It felt like my life had come full circle.

After that trip, my father and I discussed strategies on which properties to bid on for the August sale. With limited funds, my father quickly ruled out anything in the A-class neighborhoods and suggested I focus on C-class areas with a lot of potential.

In our business, cash is king; without real capital, you can't play with the big players. The game you want to play is leverage. Luckily, this concept came easily to me because of my dad's experience and my exposure to it on the corporate level. The hard part was finding investors. Private lenders are not to be confused with hard money lenders. Private lenders provide what's often called "love money," coming from family and friends with whom you have personal relationships. As a new investor, asking people to take a chance on you, especially with no experience, leads to a lot of self-doubt and fear.

Up until that point in my life, I had been reading a lot of self-help books to condition my mind to think more positively and believe in myself. It's crucial to sharpen your mindset, especially for aspiring entrepreneurs, because this is the foundation that will take you further in both your professional and personal life. With that being said, I finally got the courage to ask my immediate family members (Mom and Dad) and my fiancée (now wife) to pool our money together so I could go out and bid on our behalf.

On the day of the auction, the atmosphere was tense and electric. The courthouse steps were crowded with experienced investors, first-timers like me, and even spectators just there to witness the action. Some bidders had camped out with their lawn chairs, clearly veterans of the process, ready for a long day of bidding wars. I had my eyes on a few properties. When it finally got around to a property on my list, the opening bid was around $3,000, and my max bid was $30,000. I had been waiting for this moment for months. The auctioneer read off the terms and started the opening bid. I jumped in at around $15,000 and kept my hand raised until I was the successful bidder at $27,000. I was ecstatic, feeling the satisfaction of hard work paying off. I called my family with the great news, and we shared a moment to reflect on my thoughts and feelings throughout the whole process.

However, it was a bittersweet moment because I still had to wait until the confirmation hearing, held a couple of months after the auction. This period also gave the owner one last chance to reclaim their property by paying the back taxes. In my case, the owner showed up, and the judge gave them one final opportunity to pay the back taxes—which they did. It wasn't a loss looking back at it, but the competitor in me wanted to win. We play to win the game.

Despite the outcome, the experience taught me invaluable lessons. It wasn't just about the property; it was about the journey and the growth it sparked in me. From that day forward, my outlook on real estate and my approach to life would never be the same.

CHAPTER 8

My First Auction

– Wesley Barney

In 1993, I remember purchasing my first mortgage foreclosure property at the courthouse steps in New York City. Prior to going to auction, I invested time and money attending seminars, workshops, and reading books on foreclosure investing. I gained valuable knowledge and insight that helped me understand the foreclosure auction process. Learning the intricacies of foreclosure rules and procedures of the jurisdiction in which you plan to invest is critical for your success.

At one of the seminars I attended, the instructor suggested that we should attend foreclosure auctions as observers before participating as bidders. This allows you to watch and learn from other investors and gain a better understanding of the process without the pressure of bidding.

Getting the Foreclosure List

In purchasing my first foreclosure property at the auction, my first step was to get a list. There are several ways you can obtain a foreclosure list:

- **Subscribe to a foreclosure listing service** – Several websites specialize in providing foreclosure listings.
- **Check your local newspaper or law journal** – Every foreclosure must be published as a legal notice by law.
- **Visit courthouse records** – Public records provide details on upcoming foreclosure auctions.

I personally relied on the *New York Law Journal*, where I found legal notices titled "Notice of Foreclosure Sale" or "Pursuant to Judgment Foreclosure Sale." These notices contained critical details, including:

- Lender and owner names
- Case numbers
- Property addresses
- Legal descriptions
- Outstanding debt
- Foreclosure auction date, time, and location
- Contact information for the law firm handling the auction

What I would do next is cut out the legal notice from the newspaper and paste it in my composition book in chronological order by the date of the auction. Back in those days, we did not have iPhones, iPads, laptops, or notebooks to take screenshots of the legal notices. Wow, how times have changed! Technology has completely transformed the foreclosure business.

With the evolution from the old-school newspaper cut-and-paste method to the digital age of copy-and-paste, technology has made it much easier for real estate investors and professionals to access data and information more quickly and efficiently. Finding upcoming foreclosure auctions is just a click away.

Several companies and services specialize in publishing foreclosure auction lists. These companies often provide detailed information about upcoming foreclosure auctions, including property details, auction dates, and other relevant information. These lists are available online or through subscription services. While many online foreclosure lists strive for accuracy, it's crucial to verify the information independently. Errors or delays may occur in updating these lists, and nothing is 100% foolproof when it comes to cross-referencing information from multiple sources. Seeking legal professionals who are familiar with the foreclosure process in your area is always a smart move.

Remember, the name has changed, but the game is still the same! Adaptation to changes in the market is crucial for your success. After attending several auctions as an observer, I was ready to jump in. But before I could bid, I needed to find the right properties. That meant getting my hands on a foreclosure list and doing my due diligence.

What followed was a deep dive into researching the properties, assessing the neighborhoods, and calculating potential returns. I'll never forget the anticipation of that first bid—the thrill of the unknown and the determination to take my first step into real estate investing.

PART V

The Good with The Bad

CHAPTER 9

My Harvard Education

– Tyrek Barney

In the world of real estate, having access to capital is crucial. While traditional bank loans are a common source of funding, they often come with stringent requirements and slow approval processes. This is where private investors, such as friends and family, become invaluable. Their belief in your vision and willingness to invest can provide the financial flexibility needed to seize opportunities quickly. Additionally, consulting with a real estate attorney for legal advice is equally important. Their expertise can help navigate the complex legal landscape, ensuring that all transactions are compliant and protecting you from potential pitfalls.

This was the email I sent all my private lenders on October 15, 2021:

Exciting News:
Successful Bid on 312 Maplewood Drive!

Good Morning Everyone,

Hope everyone is having a great week and Happy Friday.

I wanted to take this time to let you know we were the successful bidder for property: 312 Maplewood Drive, Independence, MO 64050. The opening bid amount was $55k, and our winning bid was $55k! We were the only bidders!

Property details: 2 bed, 1 bath, 1,000 sq ft, Great Neighborhood. Estimated market value based on Zillow is $83k, which is not accurate because the house next door (314 Maplewood Drive) is valued at $98k with the same building structure. I believe the After Repair Value (ARV) could be in the range of $130k to $150k.

In the meantime, the next steps will be to record the deed and acquire insurance. More updates to come in the next couple of weeks. I will be heading back to KC on Oct 31st.

With that being said, thank you again to those team members who participated. Get excited!

Have a great weekend,
Tyrek Barney

You read that right, I was the only bidder at $55k! At the time of the sale, there were three investors, including myself. The other two gentlemen were competing against each other for a property prior to the one I was targeting. I enjoyed being a spectator, watching them bid this property from $30k all the way to $200k. I thought, *Wow, I need to raise more money to play with the big dawgs.* Once their battle was over, my property was next, and I was sure one of them would be my competitor.

The opening bid started at $55k, and I knew I only had $75k to play with at the time, so that was my max bid. Anxiously, I waited for the auctioneer to read off the terms. As he read the terms, the other two gentlemen were busy talking about the battle they just had, not paying attention to the current auction. The auctioneer continued to read the terms and got to the last line.

"So, the opening bid is $55,000. Do I have any offers at $55,000?" I thought there's no way I'm about to get this for $55,000, so I said, "$55,001." They were still talking to each other. The auctioneer said, "Do I have any other takers? Going once…going twice…sold to the gentleman at $55,001!" At that moment, one of the guys said, "Wait, is the bidding over? I wanted to participate." But the auctioneer replied, "It has already been sold." I stayed calm in the moment, but internally, I was ecstatic! The emotions were a rollercoaster leading up to the heat of battle, while the outcome was the opposite of what I imagined. Funny thing was, my father told me sometimes, you might be the only one bidding at the auctions. I didn't entirely believe him, but I'm a believer now!

Now that I had possession of the property, it was time to get inside and assess the condition of the home. The moment I stepped through the front door, a musty odor of damp wood and stale air hit me—this house hadn't been aired out in years. Dust particles floated through the sunlight streaming from a cracked window, illuminating cobwebs clinging to the corners of the ceiling. The floors creaked with every hesitant step, and in the kitchen, I could hear the faint sound of dripping water from a rusted faucet. Piles of debris were scattered across rooms, and the walls were discolored from years of neglect. It was clear—this house had seen better days. My father asked me what I thought it would cost to fix up. I said maybe $40k. I laugh now because that budget should've been doubled. The house needed so much work, but before I could assess the extent of the repairs, I had to clear out all the junk and get an inspection report, which I quickly did to see how much work was actually needed.

My father eventually flew to Missouri to see the property. That day, my friend and inspector, Rod, was with us to help educate and provide his professional opinion to bridge any knowledge gaps. When my father walks around silently and is busy pondering, nine times out of ten, his responses are not very positive. After reviewing the property, he approached me, nervously laughing, and told me, "This is going to be your Harvard education." Boy, he couldn't have been righter.

This project turned into an intensive learning experience. We uncovered issues that I had never anticipated—from outdated wiring and plumbing to structural concerns and hidden damages. My initial $40k estimate quickly ballooned, and I found myself knee-deep in renovations, navigating through every challenge that arose.

One of the craziest discoveries was the back-porch add-on kitchen. The previous owner had attempted to extend the kitchen by building out onto the porch, but it was a complete disaster. There were no real walls supporting the structure, and the ceiling height was a mere six feet. It was a hazard waiting to happen. We had no choice but to tear down the entire structure. Luckily, I found a contractor who was willing to take on the task of rebuilding it without permits in just three days. It was a risky move, but we needed to get it done quickly and safely.

Another unexpected twist came when I hired a siding guy to give the house a fresh look. I thought I had found a good deal, but it quickly turned into a nightmare. My electrician called me immediately to let me know that this guy had no idea how to put siding on a house correctly. The siding was crooked, and gaps were left unsealed, making the house look worse than before. I had to fire him on the spot and scramble to find someone else who could fix the mess. It was an unexpected expense and delay, but it taught me the importance of thoroughly vetting contractors

After an extensive seven-month rehab, we finally completed the house. Everything turned out beautifully, and the crew that stuck with us until the end helped us reach the finish line. With the renovations done, I aimed to sell the property quickly to capitalize on the seller's market and set my sale price around $165k. Unfortunately, by the summer of June 2022, the market had started to shift, and we received zero offers on the property that season. The clock was ticking because our loans with our private investors were coming due, and we had their money tied up in this project.

Luckily, we had an alternative exit strategy: a cash-out refinance. The property was appraised for $175k, and we pulled out 70% to pay our investors. Such a core lesson in real estate is knowing you have multiple exit strategies just in case the market takes a shift. Being adaptable in this business is critical, and that applies to business in general. We did the cash-out refinance and were able to pull enough equity from the project to pay our investors back plus their interest. Once everyone got paid out, we listed the property for rent to cover the mortgage overhead cost, and the property has been successfully rented until this day.

My father's prediction had come true: This was indeed my Harvard education. It was an education in resilience, problem-solving, and the power of a positive mindset. Every hurdle I overcame added to my knowledge and confidence, preparing me for future ventures in the world of real estate. As I look back, I am grateful for the challenges and the lessons they brought. This project was not just about one property—it was about laying the foundation for the investor I would become. Each challenge strengthened my confidence, and each lesson prepared me for bigger opportunities ahead. I didn't know it at the time, but this was only the beginning. The future held more ambitious projects, larger deals, and even greater lessons in the world of real estate. They have shaped me into a more resilient and capable investor, solidifying my determination to continue on this path, always striving for growth and excellence.

CHAPTER 10

Breaking Even

– Tyrek Barney

Every real estate project has its share of surprises, but this particular property pushed the limits of what I thought I was prepared for. While breaking even isn't the dream outcome for any investor, the experience taught me lessons in adaptability, preparation, and the value of cultivating relationships in unfamiliar territory.

This property was different from my previous investment on Maplewood Drive. Purchased at auction in August of 2024, it was located in a quiet and well-maintained neighborhood in the Kansas City, Missouri Metro Area. The area had a mix of rental properties and longtime homeowners, creating a friendly and stable community. The streets were lined with mature trees, and the houses were mostly single-family residences, each with its own unique charm. Neighbors took pride in their homes, and it was evident from the neatly trimmed lawns and freshly painted exteriors. It was the kind of neighborhood where people waved at each other in passing, and children played safely outside.

The house itself had solid bones but was the ugliest house on the block. While the rest of the neighborhood showcased well-kept homes with inviting curb appeal, this property stood out for all the wrong reasons. The paint was peeling, the siding was worn, and the overgrown yard made it look abandoned. It desperately needed a complete overhaul to match the charm of the surrounding homes.

Location is one of the most important factors in real estate, and after observing the neighborhood and evaluating the potential of this property, I had it on my radar as a promising fix-and-flip opportunity. On auction day, I arrived ready to compete. There were only two other investors bidding against me, and I watched as they battled it out. The opening bid started at $35,000, and I knew my max bid was $85,000. I strategically waited until the competition thinned out before entering the bidding. When the dust settled, I was the successful bidder at $84,500.

My plan was a full rehab and resale. I initially allocated $150,000 for acquisition and renovations, confident that with the right improvements, it could yield a strong return. However, the challenges that followed proved to be more complex than I initially anticipated. I had my reserves set aside for the inevitable bumps in the road, but reserves are meant for emergencies, not as a primary budget. What I didn't anticipate was just how extensively those reserves would be tested.

The Permit Hurdle

Early in the project, I faced an unexpected roadblock: The property had been flagged as unsafe by the city. This meant I needed to pull whole-house residential permits to move forward with renovations. Luckily, being a licensed general contractor allowed me to pull the permits in my name, saving thousands of dollars in fees that I would have otherwise paid to someone else. However, this wasn't a process I was entirely familiar with—this was my first time navigating permits in this specific city.

I quickly realized that every municipality has its own way of conducting business. From learning the city's particular permitting requirements to understanding their inspection process, it was like learning a new language. While it was frustrating at times, it was also an invaluable opportunity to create relationships with city officials, inspectors, and other key personnel in the municipality. These connections, I knew, would prove helpful for future projects in the area.

The process of pulling the permits was a crash course in patience and persistence. It required detailed submissions, back-and-forth communication, and coordination with multiple city departments. What started as a roadblock eventually became an important learning experience that added another layer of expertise to my skill set as a contractor and investor.

The Foundation Challenge

Once the permits were in place, I encountered my next hurdle: the foundation. Initial inspections revealed deeper structural issues than I had anticipated. Cracks in the foundational walls required immediate attention, and stabilization was non-negotiable. To address the problem, we installed 15 steel I-beams to support the walls and used epoxy injections to seal the cracks. The repair totaled $10,000—a significant expense that dipped into my reserve funds.

While I had planned for the possibility of foundational repairs, the extent of the work still caught me off guard. It was a stark reminder of why reserves are crucial, even though relying on them so early in the process was not ideal.

The Sewer Line Surprise

Just as I thought the worst was behind me, the sewer line threw another wrench into the plan. The curb box, essential for shutting off water to the property, had been destroyed by roots from a tree planted by the city decades ago. This required a complete replacement.

Additionally, the sewer line itself had a break eight feet from the house. Fortunately, we only needed a spot repair instead of replacing the entire line—a small relief in an otherwise expensive project. Together, these plumbing repairs added another $10,000 to the budget.

The Learning Curve and Relationships

The foundation and sewer issues were critical but manageable. However, navigating the permitting process and working with a new municipality was a completely different challenge. Being unfamiliar with their systems, I spent extra time understanding their requirements and protocols. Building relationships with city officials and inspectors was a key part of the process. While it slowed progress initially, these connections laid the groundwork for smoother operations in future projects.

In hindsight, being a licensed general contractor was a major advantage. If I had to rely on a third party to pull permits, I would have incurred additional costs and delays. This experience reinforced the value of having the right credentials and skill set to manage unexpected situations efficiently.

Revisiting the Budget

With these unexpected repairs and permit challenges, the renovation costs ballooned to $175,000, exceeding the original budget by $25,000. Once the property was market-ready, we listed it for $225,000, optimistic about its potential. However, the real estate market had shifted, with rising interest rates and fewer buyers. After weeks of little interest, I reduced the asking price to $195,000 to attract buyers.

Closing the Deal

The price reduction worked, and we eventually secured a buyer. However, closing the deal incurred additional costs, including $14,791.70 in agent commissions, seller concessions, and title fees.

Lessons Learned

In the end, we broke even—not the result I had hoped for, but one that left me with these invaluable lessons:

- **Preparation and Flexibility:** While I had reserves for unexpected repairs, the foundation and sewer issues highlighted the importance of being flexible with financial planning. Reserves are essential but should be preserved whenever possible.
- **Navigating Permitting Processes:** Learning to work within a new city's permitting system and building relationships with key personnel is an investment in smoother operations for future projects.
- **The Value of Being Licensed:** My general contractor license saved me significant time and money during the permitting process. This credential proved to be a crucial advantage in overcoming project delays.
- **Adapting to Market Conditions:** The reduced sale price was a tough but necessary decision to close the deal in a shifting market. Adapting quickly is critical to minimizing losses.

- **Multiple Exit Strategies:** Breaking even, while not ideal, is better than a loss. Having options like refinancing or renting can provide a safety net in challenging market conditions.

Looking Ahead

This project tested my skills, patience, and ability to adapt. While it didn't generate a profit, it left me better prepared for the challenges of future investments. Breaking even is never the goal, but it's part of the reality of real estate investing. The experience reinforced the importance of preparation, adaptability, and maintaining strong relationships—both in business and with municipal partners.

As I plan my next projects, I carry these lessons forward, knowing they will guide me toward greater success. Real estate isn't just about profit; it's about growth, resilience, and turning every challenge into an opportunity for improvement.

PART VI

Advanced Strategies & Lessons

CHAPTER 11

Mastering Trustee Sales

– Wesley Barney

In the unpredictable world of real estate, where deals are made and fortunes rise and fall, few events rival the excitement and intrigue of trustee foreclosure sales. I vividly recall the scene back in 2002 when New York City foreclosure auctions typically drew a modest crowd of around five investors. Fast forward to today, and the landscape has dramatically shifted, with auctions now attracting a highly competitive throng of ten to fifteen eager bidders, driving prices upward and leading to overbidding on properties.

During my time attending real estate club meetings in New York, I met an investor who was curious about opportunities in Kansas City since I had already been there. She was eager to learn more about trustee sales and was intrigued by my experience in the market. As we discussed strategies, she expressed interest in becoming involved financially. Recognizing the opportunity, she decided to partner with me as a money partner, providing capital to fund our first trustee sale investment together. This partnership gave us the flexibility to pursue properties that might have been out of reach individually, allowing us to make strategic moves in Kansas City. As we explored investment opportunities outside of New York, I set my sights on KC. One winter, I flew out to Kansas City for my first trustee sale. Before attending the auction, I did my usual due diligence—researching the property, assessing its location, and conducting an exterior inspection. While walking around the property, I met a friendly neighbor who was eager to share insights. He informed me that the home had been neglected by its previous owner, which gave me valuable intel about its history and potential renovation needs.

When auction day arrived, I made my way to the courthouse steps. The opening bid for the property I had my eye on was $35,000. I scanned the crowd, expecting a competitive bidding war, but to my surprise, no other investors showed up. As the auctioneer read the terms of the sale, I kept looking around, waiting for someone else to jump in. When no one did, I placed my bid, and just like that, I became the successful—and only—bidder at $35,100. I couldn't believe it. The excitement and disbelief of winning a property with no competition left a lasting impression on me. This experience solidified my belief that Kansas City trustee sales had untapped potential for real estate investors willing to explore new markets.

Why Trustee Sales Are Worth Pursuing

A trustee foreclosure auction is a type of foreclosure sale where a trustee, typically appointed by the lender, oversees the auction process. This is usually handled by an attorney or law firm instead of the courts. If the borrower defaults for more than 90 days on their mortgage payments, the trustee has the authority to sell the property at a public oral bid auction to the highest bidder for all cash. It's a way for the lender to expedite the foreclosure process and recover the outstanding debt owed.

Trustee sales have several advantages over traditional foreclosures:

- **Speed of Purchase:** Unlike judicial foreclosures, which can take months or even years to process through the courts, trustee sales happen quickly, allowing investors to acquire properties without long waiting periods.
- **Fewer Legal Hurdles:** Since trustee sales bypass the court system, the process is more streamlined, reducing bureaucratic delays.
- **Potential for Lower Prices:** Many properties are sold below market value, providing opportunities for investors to acquire assets at a discount.

Of course, trustee sales also come with challenges. There's little to no opportunity to inspect the property beforehand, and the transactions are all cash. However, with thorough research and a well-thought-out strategy, these auctions can be a goldmine for investors willing to take calculated risks.

Expanding My Trustee Sale Strategy

After my initial success, I knew trustee sales were a strategy worth pursuing long-term. Over the years, I refined my approach, learning how to spot the best deals, build relationships with key contacts, and mitigate risks. Investing in trustee sales has become one of my most reliable methods for acquiring properties, and I continue to use this strategy as a cornerstone of my real estate business.

Looking back, making the transition from New York City foreclosure auctions to trustee sales in Kansas City was one of the best decisions I ever made. It opened new doors, expanded my investing reach, and provided me with a more efficient way to grow my portfolio. Trustee sales remain one of the most exciting and rewarding aspects of real estate investing, and for those who are willing to put in the effort, they can be an incredible wealth-building tool.

CHAPTER 12

The Value of Education

– Wesley Barney

When I got started investing in real estate, I purchased many books and home study courses, listened to tapes, attended many seminars, workshops, weekend boot camps, and real estate investing conferences, joined local real estate investors groups, and networked with like-minded people. One of the keys to being a successful real estate investor is to find your niche, an area that you would like to specialize in. You don't want to be a jack of all trades and a master of none!

Most of my family, friends, business associates, and students know I specialize in buying foreclosure properties at the auction. That is my go-to move, and it works for me. Now, don't get me wrong, it is good to have an understanding of how to do other types of real estate transactions because you never know when an opportunity comes knocking at your door. You want to be prepared to seize the opportunity.

In my own case, I remember one time I was driving around in Brooklyn, New York, and ran across a vacant property. I researched who the owner was and mailed them a letter expressing my interest in buying their property. The daughter called me and explained that her mother was in a nursing home, and she had the power of attorney. The family was interested in selling the house. She told me that if I wanted to see the inside of the house, she would drive down to Brooklyn over the weekend to let me see it.

I met her over the weekend, looked around the house, and it was in relatively good shape. The house was a two-story, row-style brick house. The roof, foundation, windows, and plumbing were intact. The heating system needed an upgrade, and the electrical panel was good. The property just needed some cleaning up, paint, and plaster. I told her I liked the property and would make her an offer later in the day. I contacted her and made an offer of $50,000. She asked, "Can you do $55,000?" I said yes and explained that I would have my attorney draw up the contract and forward it to her attorney. The property was free and clear with no mortgage. The comps in the area revealed that the market value of the property was about $125,000.

Now, I did not have $55,000 cash to purchase the building. However, I had my attorney put a clause in the contract that I could assign this contract to a third party, and I would have 30 days to close on the property. I notified my real estate broker friend who buys and sells real estate in that area. I told him about the property that I had under contract. The daughter left an extra key with the next-door neighbor. My broker friend and I looked inside the property, and he liked it. I told him he could purchase it from me for $65,000. My contract price was $55,000. Of course, he haggled the price down to $63,000. I said okay. I put him in contact with my attorney.

To make a long story short, he closed on the property. I made an extra $8,000 minus my attorney fee and closing costs, and I put no money in the deal. This transaction would not have been possible if I had not taken the real estate seminar and workshop on how to spot abandoned properties and assign contracts. I would have walked right past this opportunity. However, these deals don't come along every day, but when they do, you need to be ready to seize the opportunity.

PART VII

Wisdom for Future Generations

CHAPTER 13

Core Principles

– Tyrek and Wesley Barney

As we look back on our journey, certain principles and values stand out as the foundation of our success. Integrity, perseverance, and continuous learning have been our guiding lights. We believe that success is not just about financial gain but also about making a positive impact on the community and leaving a lasting legacy.

Integrity is non-negotiable. In every deal, every negotiation, and every interaction, maintaining honesty and transparency has built trust with our partners, investors, and clients. Perseverance has seen us through the toughest times, and continuous learning has kept us adaptable and innovative.

For those looking to embark on a real estate journey, we offer this advice:

1. **Educate Yourself:** Invest time in learning about the industry. Read books, attend seminars, and seek out mentors.

2. **Network:** Build relationships with other investors, real estate professionals, and potential partners. Networking opens doors to opportunities and valuable insights.

3. **Start Small:** Begin with manageable projects and gradually scale up as you gain experience and confidence.
4. **Be Persistent:** Real estate investing is not without challenges. Stay determined, learn from setbacks, and keep moving forward.
5. **Have Multiple Exit Strategies:** Always plan for various outcomes to ensure flexibility and adaptability.
6. **Invest in Yourself:** Continuous self-improvement is crucial. Develop your skills, mindset, and knowledge base.

Real estate is more than just buying and selling properties; it is about creating opportunities, building communities, and securing financial independence. Whether you're just starting out or already deep in the game, these principles will guide you. Stay honest and stay ready for whatever comes next. Because in this business, the only limit is the one you set for yourself. We hope that by sharing our journey, we can inspire and equip others with the tools and knowledge needed to succeed. The road ahead may not always be smooth, but with the right principles and mindset, success is within reach.

CHAPTER 14

Real Estate Investors Association

– Wesley Barney

My journey into real estate investing began in the early 1990s, sparked by a late-night infomercial on television. The message was simple yet powerful: "You too can be rich through real estate investing!" That single phrase lit a fire in me, and I thought, *Why not me?* Determined to change my circumstances, I purchased countless books and tapes on the subject, immersing myself in the world of real estate investing.

Each book brought me closer to understanding the ins and outs of the industry. I absorbed the knowledge like a sponge, rewinding and replaying those tapes over and over until the lessons became second nature. These tapes became my personal mentors, guiding me through concepts that would later become the foundation of my success.

One day, while reading one of these real estate books, I came across a chapter that emphasized the importance of joining a local real estate club. Intrigued, I researched where I could find one and discovered the Creative Investors of America (CIA) in New York City, run by Jay Dyer. Little did

I know that this decision would propel my real estate investing career forward. Joining this local real estate club allowed me to connect with like-minded individuals who shared my passion for real estate. It became the starting point for building relationships with fellow investors, agents, and enthusiasts ready to share their experiences.

The Power of Networking

The true power of networking became apparent to me during those monthly meetings. Each gathering was an opportunity to chat with members, exchange contact information, and build relationships with both seasoned investors and newcomers like myself. These connections became invaluable, leading to partnerships, mentorships, and potential investment opportunities.

To this day, I maintain relationships with investors I met at those monthly meetings, some of whom are still my real estate partners and close friends over two decades later. Networking wasn't just about creating business connections; it was about building a community of people who supported and challenged each other to grow.

Sharing Knowledge

One of the most significant benefits of being part of a real estate club was the immense wealth of knowledge available. Each meeting featured guest speakers, workshops, seminars, field trips, and discussions on a wide range of real estate topics.

I gained insights into:

- Market trends
- Financing options
- Foreclosures
- Rehabbing properties
- Private lending
- Wholesaling and assignment of contracts
- Rental property management
- Multifamily investing
- Setting up LLCs, land trusts, and asset protection strategies
- Negotiation tactics

Hearing real-life experiences from other members was invaluable. Their stories of success and failure helped me avoid common pitfalls and develop a more refined approach to investing. It was a masterclass in real estate investing, delivered by people who were walking the walk.

Support and Motivation

Real estate investing isn't always glamorous. It can be stressful, lonely, and full of uncertainty. But the camaraderie of the club members made the journey far more enjoyable. Members celebrated each other's achievements and provided guidance and encouragement during tough times. The sense of accountability within the group inspired me to stay focused and committed to my goals.

There was a time when I was struggling to find partners to join me in purchasing a real estate investment. I attended a real estate networking meeting, going around the room to see if anyone was interested in partnering on an apartment project. Eventually, I spoke to someone who referred me to their contact. Over the next two months, I developed a business relationship with this new contact, and they ultimately became one of my partners in buying a six-family apartment building. This experience solidified the power of networking and the importance of persistence in finding the right opportunities and, more importantly, the right people.

Having this community wasn't just about gaining knowledge—it was about finding a support system. The emotional and moral support I received from my fellow members made all the difference during moments of doubt or challenge.

Access to Resources

Another major advantage of being part of a real estate club was access to a treasure trove of resources. Within the club, I discovered reliable:

- Contractors
- Property managers
- Attorneys
- Title companies
- Insurance brokers
- Real estate agents
- Mortgage brokers
- Bankers

Fellow members were always happy to recommend professionals they had worked with successfully, saving me time and energy in my search for trustworthy partners. Additionally, the club provided opportunities to learn about properties for sale by investors and potential deals that weren't listed on the open market.

Building Your Own Community

By joining a real estate investors association, I gained much more than just education—I gained a network, resources, and long-term partnerships that helped shape my career. This decision remains one of the most impactful choices I ever made in my journey as an investor.

For those looking to follow a similar path, I highly encourage you to seek out a local real estate club, an online group, or a circle of like-minded investors. Surrounding yourself with people who share your goals and ambitions will accelerate your growth, provide you with new opportunities, and create a lasting support system. In this business, success isn't just about what you know—it's also about who you know.

PART VIII

Building a Winning Team

CHAPTER 15

Teamwork Makes the Dream Work

– Tyrek and Wesley Barney

Building your real estate team is like being the owner of a sports team franchise—you carefully select your managers, coaches, and players. Each member of your team brings different talents and skill sets, and their ability to work together creates a winning outcome for you, the owner. You know you cannot do it alone—no one can. Real estate is no different; you need to seek out players and coaches to help you achieve your investment goals. Real estate is a relationship business.

Here is the list of our essential real estate team members. Your list may differ based on your experience and where you are in your investment career:

- Real estate agents
- Attorneys
- CPA accountants
- Contractors

- Investment partners
- Title companies
- Property managers
- Insurance brokers

Real Estate Agents

A knowledgeable real estate agent understands local market trends, property values, and neighborhood dynamics, ensuring that you make informed decisions. We recommend finding an agent in the area where you plan to invest. A good agent has access to multiple listing services as well as off-market properties available for purchase. Experienced agents are skilled negotiators who can help secure the best price and terms, whether you're buying or selling. They often have a network of professionals, like contractors and title companies, which can be invaluable.

Skilled agents can also keep you on their buyers' list for investment opportunities that align with your strategies. A dedicated real estate agent can be one of the most valuable assets on your team.

Real Estate Attorneys

It is imperative to develop a relationship with a local real estate attorney. This person can be worth their weight in gold. You can find attorneys through local bar associations, real estate investment groups, or online directories.

A real estate attorney provides guidance on contracts, laws, and regulations, helping you avoid legal issues. In disputes, they can negotiate settlements or represent you in court. Attorneys assist with asset protection by setting up LLCs or trusts to ensure generational wealth and help with closing transactions to ensure documents are executed properly.

We recommend hiring an attorney who specializes in real estate law rather than a generalist. Good attorneys may charge more, but their expertise will save you money and headaches in the long run. Interview several attorneys to find the right fit for your team.

Certified Public Accountants (CPA)

A CPA specializing in real estate tax laws can help you maximize deductions (like depreciation) and minimize tax liabilities. They assist with budgeting, cash flow forecasting, and financial planning, ensuring your investments align with your financial goals.

If you're rehabbing and flipping properties regularly, a CPA becomes essential for managing your tax strategies. They can also keep you informed about changing tax laws and advise on the best business structure to protect your assets.

Remember, taxes are one of life's guarantees, and a good CPA ensures you're always prepared.

General Contractors (GC)

If you lack experience with property repairs, a general contractor is essential to your team, especially for rehab projects. Skilled contractors bring years of experience in areas like plumbing, carpentry, and electrical work. They understand building codes, permits, and best practices, ensuring projects run smoothly and legally.

A good contractor saves time and money by leveraging relationships with suppliers and subcontractors for better pricing. Their problem-solving skills prevent delays and keep projects on track.

Having an experienced contractor as part of your team outweighs the risks of attempting to do it all yourself.

Investment Partners

Private lenders are the unsung heroes of real estate investment, providing flexible funding that traditional banks can't match. They allow you to act quickly on opportunities, especially at foreclosure auctions where immediate payment is often required.

Unlike traditional lenders, private lenders offer flexible terms on interest rates, repayment schedules, and collateral. They are often everyday people—family, friends, coworkers, or business associates—seeking higher returns on their capital.

Private lenders are the fairy godparents of your real estate journey, providing the magic capital to fund your projects. Just remember—they expect a little magic in return. However, working with private investors comes with responsibilities and risks. To ensure a successful partnership, consider these key precautions:

- **Have Written Agreements:** Clearly outline the terms of the partnership, including interest rates, repayment schedules, and any equity splits.
- **Define Repayment Terms:** Set clear expectations regarding when and how the investor will be paid back.
- **Ensure Legal Protection:** Work with an attorney to draft legal agreements to protect both parties.
- **Manage Investor Expectations:** Be transparent about risks, timelines, and potential setbacks.
- **Verify Investor Reliability:** Just as investors vet you, you should also vet them to ensure they are trustworthy and financially capable.

By taking these steps, you can establish strong, mutually beneficial relationships with private investors while mitigating potential pitfalls.

Title Companies

Title companies play a vital role in real estate transactions. They conduct title searches to verify ownership and identify potential liens or claims. They provide title insurance, protecting buyers and lenders from legal disputes.

These companies also coordinate the closing process, prepare essential documents, and handle fund disbursements to ensure transactions run smoothly. A reliable title company is indispensable for every property you purchase.

Property Managers

Property managers ensure the smooth day-to-day operation of your investment properties. Their duties include tenant communication, rent collection, financial management, and legal compliance with local and federal regulations.

They work tirelessly to minimize vacancies, handle tenant complaints, and juggle multiple responsibilities to keep your properties profitable. In short, they ensure your investment stays afloat.

Insurance Brokers

Insurance brokers are the backbone of your team, providing peace of mind by securing tailored coverage for your properties. They understand the nuances of insurance policies, ensuring you're adequately protected based on your property's location, value, and risks.

Brokers streamline the search process, advocate during claims, and recommend specific policies for vacant properties, new construction, or rental properties. Their expertise saves you time and ensures your investments are well-protected.

CONCLUSION

No matter your investment level—whether you're a novice or an experienced investor—you'll eventually need a few seasoned pros on your team to navigate the complexities of real estate. These team members are the foundation of your success, ensuring your journey is as smooth and profitable as possible. So, build your dream team wisely, because in real estate, like in sports, championships aren't won alone.

Reflecting on the journey, we recognize the importance of legacy and the future of our real estate endeavors. For us, legacy isn't just about the wealth we accumulate but the knowledge, values, and opportunities we pass down to future generations. It's about helping others build financial security, foster economic independence, and make a lasting impact in our communities. Real estate is more than a business; it's a vehicle for empowerment and generational success.

So, stay curious, stay committed, and most importantly, take action. Your real estate story is waiting to be written. Go make it happen.

RESOURCES & FURTHER LEARNING

Thank you for joining us on this journey. Real estate investing is a continuous learning process, and having the right tools and connections can make all the difference. Below are some resources to help you take the next step in your own investment journey.

Stay Connected

📌 www.Tjinvestors.com

Books We Recommend

- *Rich Dad Poor Dad* by Robert Kiyosaki
- *How to Raise Capital for Real Estate Legally* by Kim Lisa Taylor, ESQ
- *The Magic of Thinking Big* by David Schwartz
- *Acres Of Diamonds* by, Russell Conwell
- *How to Win Friends and Influence People* by Dale Carnegie
- *See you at The Top* by Zig Zeller
- *It's Not Over until you win* by Les Brown
- *171 ways to make money in Real Estate* by Sonny Block
- *The courage to be Rich* by Mark O. Haroldsen

- *Real Estate for Pennies on the Dollar* by John Beck
- *Tax Sales, Tax Certificates the Unknown Wealth Builder* by Harry Friedland

Online Resources & Communities

- BiggerPockets (biggerpockets.com) – A great forum for real estate investors of all levels.
- Local Real Estate Investment Associations (REIAs) – Search for a real estate investment club in your area.

Have Questions? Want to Learn More?

Stay connected with us! Visit www.Tjinvestors.com to learn more about our latest projects, investment opportunities, and insights into real estate investing.

ACKNOWLEDGEMENTS

Wesley Barney:
To my beloved grandparents, Ameila "Moniz" Debrause and Joseph Wesley Debrause, whose limited education never hindered their wisdom. Thank you for instilling in me a strong work ethic and deep love for family. Your unwavering support and values guide me every day.

To my family, friends, investors, and mentors—your belief in us and our vision has made this journey possible. We couldn't have done it without you.

This book is dedicated to those who have ever been told they can't do it. Success is built on persistence, learning from failures, and pushing forward despite obstacles. May this serve as a blueprint for those striving to build something greater for themselves, their families, and their communities.

Tyrek Barney:
To my parents, who showed me the value of hard work, resilience, and believing in something bigger than myself. Your sacrifices paved the way for opportunities I don't take for granted. Every challenge I've faced, every lesson I've learned, is a reflection of the foundation you built for me.

To the investors, mentors, and friends who have been part of my journey—your support has been instrumental in shaping my path. Whether through guidance, partnership, or simply a word of encouragement, you've helped turn ideas into reality.

To those chasing something greater—whether it's financial freedom, personal growth, or a dream others may not understand—this book is for you. The road isn't always easy, but the journey is worth it. Keep moving forward, keep taking risks, and trust that every lesson, even the difficult ones, will bring you closer to your goals.

CONNECT WITH THE BARNEYS

www.TJInvestors.com

Wesley Barney | BunkeyBarney@gmail.com
Tyrek Barney | TyrekBarney@gmail.com

ABOUT THE AUTHORS

Wesley Barney is a seasoned real estate investor, author, publisher of *How to Invest in Tax Delinquent Properties*, and public speaker with over 20 years of experience specializing in tax lien properties, tax deeds, and foreclosures. As the founder and president of Ultimate Investors Real Estate Inc., he has successfully navigated markets in New York City, Syracuse, Kansas City, and Tulsa, identifying undervalued properties and transforming them into profitable opportunities.

Bravely, Mr. Barney has retired from the New York City Fire Department after 25 years of service. His career highlights include serving as a contributing editor for Creative Real Estate Magazine and as an instructor for continuing adult education programs at St. John's University, Queens Community College, and the Learning Annex. His expertise was nationally recognized when he appeared in John Beck's influential late-1990s infomercial on tax-delinquent properties, cementing his reputation as a trusted voice in real estate investing.

Wesley's mission is to empower the next generation of investors through real-world knowledge, strategic insight, and a commitment to legacy-building.

* * *

Tyrek Barney is a real estate investor, corporate professional, and emerging voice in the world of entrepreneurship. Balancing a successful career in corporate finance with his passion for real estate, Tyrek has developed a strategic approach to investing, specializing in foreclosures, distressed properties, and renovation projects. His investment journey spans diverse markets, particularly Kansas City, Missouri, where he's established a track record of identifying opportunities and overcoming challenges.

With a strong foundation rooted in both corporate experience and hands-on real estate ventures, Tyrek uniquely bridges analytical insight with practical application. His collaborative spirit, coupled with a commitment to personal growth and financial literacy, positions him as a relatable mentor and role model for aspiring entrepreneurs and investors.

Tyrek's mission is to inspire others to embrace entrepreneurship, build financial independence, and create lasting legacies through disciplined investing and purposeful action.

www.ingramcontent.com/pod-product-compliance
Ingram Content Group UK Ltd.
Pitfield, Milton Keynes, MK11 3LW, UK
UKHW021606110926
15112UKWH00017B/91

9 798218 640279